THE MONSTER I AM TODAY

THE MONSTER I AM TODAY
LEONTYNE PRICE AND A LIFE IN VERSE

KEVIN SIMMONDS

TriQuarterly Books/Northwestern University Press
Evanston, Illinois

TriQuarterly Books
Northwestern University Press
www.nupress.northwestern.edu

Individual poems and prose excerpts have appeared in *Crazyhorse, Foglifter, Lana Turner Journal, Poetry,* and *World Literature Today.*

This work combines fiction and nonfiction. Apart from direct quotes and actual events, the voices and situations of Leontyne Price and the other characters are fictional. My high school voice teacher's name has been changed.

Printed in the United States of America

10   9   8   7   6   5   4   3   2   1

Library of Congress Cataloging-in-Publication Data

Names: Simmonds, Kevin, author.
Title: The monster I am today : Leontyne Price and a life in verse / Kevin
    Simmonds.
Description: Evanston, Illinois : TriQuarterly Books/Northwestern University Press,
    2021. | Includes bibliographical references.
Identifiers: LCCN 2020055886 | ISBN 9780810143746 (paperback) | ISBN
    9780810143753 (ebook)
Subjects: LCSH: Price, Leontyne—Poetry. | African American musicians—Poetry. |
    African American gay men—Poetry.
Classification: LCC PS3619.I5576 M66 2021 | DDC 811.6—dc23
LC record available at https://lccn.loc.gov/2020055886

CONTENTS

her face & chest

low-lit

black gown

square-necked & sequined

sleeves

of beaded fringe

The United Negro College Fund commercial
where she sang

We're not asking for a handout, just a hand!

1984

Leontyne Price
(born February 10, 1927)

I discovered in her whirling howl my human noise
my instrument eye

OVERTURE

January 3, 1985

Aida, act 3

The oboe spirals. Clarinets sway.

"Mai più!"—she will "never again" see home. This princess slave, this Ethiopian.

Wielding her arsenal Black body, Price calibrates, smokes the middle.

Her ascent to high C, then down the key's triad. Nearly 17 seconds on a single breath.

When I sang Aida, my skin was my costume.

She finishes how she'd refused to begin

> *Leontyne is to be a great artist. She is to be one of the greats.*
> *When she makes her debut at the Met, she must do it as a lady,*
> *not a slave.*
>
> Peter Herman Adler

She extinguishes the high A to ovation

0:16   *Furrows brow*

0:19   *Steadies composure*

1:26   *Lowers head and begins to cry, shoulders shake*

1:43   *Lifts head, composed*

2:07   *Lowers head*

2:12   *Lifts head and takes two deep breaths*

2:17   *Falls to knees, head high*

2:26   *Rests hands on chest*

2:43   *Lowers head*

2:53   *Stands*

3:03   *Lowers head and moves stage left*

3:06   *Ovation ends*

For three riotous minutes, the entire evening becomes *her* story.

The Metropolitan Opera's first Black singer of belonging, the first to sing *multiple* leading roles.

The 42-minute ovation—still the house record—for her debut as Leonora in Verdi's *Il Trovatore*.

24 years. 42 times as Aida. More than 200 performances.

A single camera fills its frame. Pain, relief, vindication surface upon her face.

My 12-year-old body can hardly bear the recognition—*this* is what I want: adulation.

The sound we recognize as *operatic* is absolute. It journeys on breath—rationed and shaped through the torso, neck, mouth and face—and arrives *loud* to resound over grand orchestras of vibrating woods and metals.

The operatic voice exits the body a procession of elemental sonances: hard, liquid, gauzy, molten. Winged with vowel, words glint, irradiated.

This human sound dazzles and falters. Even a single note may waver in stature. Beyond the beauty of tone and shapeliness of phrase, there's an understanding of material, architecture and weather.

An aria is a weather event. The singer and listener experience how the voice creates the conditions and withstands its forces. Together they determine the weather.

Before any human, wooden or metal vibration, they consent to a *being-there*. To contract and enlarge, to vanish and return.

The pressures and temperatures of expectation also vary. Thus, the primordial weather, the frisson.

The opera singer conceals, much like a ballerina, the work it takes to appear effortless. Yet she is without a floor to absorb any misstep. She must make the floor—her body is the floor.

I never cared for the plots: rich-people problems patter-sung in drawing rooms and boudoirs, the bloated verismo of tubercular peasants, kidnappings and uprisings, suicides and mad scenes.

Opera: Italian for "a work, a labor"; the feminine Latin root *op*: "to work, produce in abundance."

Feminine work of abundance—that's what I sought to behold and to become.

The first time my friend Brian called her "Pri-ce" (Pre-chay), I hollered. Dizzied by her wallop, queens are wont to add a second syllable to *rev*.

La voce, feminine. To penetrate a queer man as only a woman can.

Not Maria Callas or Birgit Nilsson. Not Anita Baker or Janet Jackson. Not Jennifer Holliday or Bernadette Peters.

Patti LaBelle and Kathleen Battle came close.

One pierced with the fitful force of her own possession, her guttural trance. The other angelic, fallen, whiplash coloratura contorting her small mouth (the one she famously demanded other performers *not* to look at).

Enraptured as I was by the North Star of Luther Vandross, I regarded him as I did the gospel great Raymond Myles and others like him: showboating sissies garish in their Sunday getups and Jheri curls, flaunting their breathy falsetto. Although my sound was nothing like theirs, I knew we were kin.

Whenever Michael Jackson appeared on TV, my cousin Cherie became hysterical, believing he'd become incarnate *for her*. And never more than when *Thriller* premiered on MTV (December 2, 1983).

With her convulsing on its edge, Momma's bed collapsed, spilling Cherie and us (Aunt Trina, Cousin Lauren and me) onto the floor. Face red and swollen, Cherie laugh-wept without once taking her eyes off of Michael transforming into a monster.

Right then, I swore off teen idolatry. I'd remain solemn as when the priests raised the Host and, on my knees, I rang the bells—altar boy full of shame.

When Ms. Bragg asked our 7th grade Life Science class if we knew about AIDS, Wilbert Gilmore shouted, "That's the disease fags get!"

His certainty was a relief: there were others whose nature was killing them.

I'd always thought I needed to grow an *extremity* so magnificent I'd be forgiven my nature, redeemed for being Black and gay, ordinary.

I grew up with only braggadocio and brawn to measure against the treble of my quivering and wide-eyed softness. Weighed down down by the same fear the men and boys of my neighborhood inherited from kin

—and skin—

so I emptied emptied to fill with unbelonging and dread—enough to deform me

Kevin, you're hungry because you've never been fed.

Wilbert had given me a name and brotherhood of the dead and dying, so I fixated on his veined forearms and biceps, his quarterback thighs and calves, as I rubbed against the underside of my desk, emptying emptying to make room enough for the virus, its prognosis and whatever else he'd feed me.

After I whispered, "I think I'm gay," to Mrs. Stewart the school counselor, she smiled, led me to her office and handed me a tape collection of Dr. Leo Buscaglia. I didn't know what to make of this middle-aged Italian man whose cheery admonitions convinced throngs of PBS subscribers to love themselves, but I knew Mrs. Stewart had shown me a tremendous kindness.

Trapped in the terror of Mississippi segregation, Price's family and community nurtured her voice (and pianistic talents) as both a *calling* and means to a stable life as a teacher. Making family and community proud was indistinguishable from uplifting the race.

Neither family nor community saw my talent as a divine calling. It held promise—that was it. Absent their enthusiasm and certainty about my future in classical music, my self-edict was to epitomize excellence, which seemed to require disavowing and *overcoming* Blackness to achieve it.

Kevin, you're sick because you're so hungry.

New Orleans, 7th ward, the clapboard house Great Grandfather built. Me, Momma and stepfather Willie who drawled his double negatives and stank of one-note cologne, the supposed upgrade from my cheating, ever-smiling Jamaican father with gold rims and a star in his mouth, a way for Momma to trade her 9-to-5 at the welfare office for 19" Zeniths to watch nonstop in almost every room: soap operas like *As the World Turns*, talk shows like *Donahue*, the five-o'clock news, dramas like *Dallas*, *Dynasty* and *Hill Street Blues*, the 10 o'clock news, late-night talk shows like *The Tonight Show*, late-night news like *Nightline*, late-late-night reruns like her all-time favorite, *The Twilight Zone*.

She devoted her attention to whatever seemed farthest from our life on North Galvez Street. Aliens, her most distant fixation, menaced me.

ABDUCTION

That Momma claims she saw a UFO while waiting at the bus stop is not what worries me. It's her waiting with the TV on since that childhood sighting. She expects some sign. A wink inside the late-night infomercial. Then return.

If I had syringe-long fingers. If I shimmered instead of spoke. If my filament glowed in the dark and blackness pooled in my irises. Maybe then she'd look at me, smile and say, *I knew you'd come.*

Unable to make sense of his wife's condition or how to raise a sissy who so despised him, Willie ran the streets. Willie "Bob" who'd worked offshore for months at a time, who relied on muscle to move things and people, who, disabled by a work injury, squandered Momma's money on liquor and weed.

With bloodshot eyes and a bass voice he used as sledgehammer, he'd threaten to "put a hurting" on me.

Eight years old, in a house without anyone to bear witness, to shape the only child. No provisions to foster my interests, because neither Momma nor Willie ever observed long enough, or with sufficient attention, to discern the obvious curiosities of a child, much less the hints announced in my ruses of nonchalance.

Or they didn't care.

Yet I looked to them for assurances, as any child would. And they made little impression besides to intensify my ambitions—resentments, really, that they did nothing I wanted to emulate.

On the occasional Sunday afternoon, the house shook with LPs and 45s—a sabbath for Momma who'd long ago fled from Mass and the schoolhouse nuns. She danced from living room to kitchen. "Turn it up, Kevin! Turn it up!"

Hey
hey hey hey
hey Pockey A-way

These eyes have seen a lot of loves but they're never gonna see
another one like I had with you

Brother, brother, brother
there's far too many of you dying

I didn't want these afternoons to end. Momma was mine, not cloistered in her room, lost inside a soap. Eyes on me and fingers snapping, she sang songs that had gotten her through—but not *away*.

I rummaged her collection to find how I'd need to sound—to *leave* that house. As I began assembling my own, I sang and sang, growing a voice that would soon outsize my frame and crystallize into a shell.

Until the end of time
I'll be there for you

Candy Girl
You are my world

Portuguese love
Won't you say it to me, say it to me, say you love me, baby

Shout, shout, let it all out
These are the things I can do without

What's love got to do, got to do with it

A curiosity, this shell deflected the disdain classmates had for my feminine ways. This confused me because I'd thought my voice gave me away, how my femininity leaked out and marked me.

As the pelting hisses of "Faggot!" and "Punk!" grew stronger, I dimmed and receded to fend off fists I knew would replace them. I could no longer avert my eyes and slouch behind the girls, my protectors.

It lasts, seeing Black men and boys as threats, humiliators.

FADE

I come nervous into the shop
of soaking instruments & talc
where I nod & drop
into a mannish grunt

Men & boys doubled
in a wall of mirrors
blunt my manner until
I'm nearly mute

He calls me to the chair above
the coiled black jetsam
gown dusted & whipped
into the cleansing air

His hands across my forehead
& down the temple
I close my eyes
against this warmth

He turns me
surveys what I can't see
asks little because he knows
to fear my kind

When I rise shaped & lined
there's no applause no dap
only the residue of what
we're willing to bear

But then, the merciful arrival for *my kind*: high school chorus.

The choir at all-Black McDonogh 35 Senior High School sang Negro spirituals like "Elijah Rock" and "Soon Ah Will Be Done," Black Creole folk songs like "Fais Do-Do" and "Monsieur Banjo," and classical standards like Bach's "Jesu, Joy of Man's Desiring" and "Commit Thy Ways, O Pilgrim."

The director, Ms. Patricia Sallier Seals, recognized my talent and nurtured it like no teacher before or since. She taught me to play piano, and I practiced in the choir room, without fail, every day during lunch and after school. I soon mastered sight-reading and bossily took classmates aside to perfect their parts. By junior year, I was accompanying the choir in performances.

From freshman year, I was a standout, a soloist. Pimply and insecure whenever I wasn't grasping a score and sounding my tremulous tones, my voice commanding attention because it asserted that striking, girth-giving oscillation: vibrato.

Its bombastic shake and naked shimmer, its self-congratulating excess. My gay adolescent dream: a voice that gave me character, or allowed me to *play* a character. Operatic.

Ms. Seals assigned me solos almost immediately, which provoked some teasing from the upperclassmen, but more than anything, endeared me to a group who had personality and pluck to spare. We weren't the perennial social rejects and losers. We had the respect and admiration of our peers. We were *fresh*.

Ms. Seals appeared to be in her 60s and displayed the poise, grace and dignity of another era, replete with meticulous, unchanging donut bun and bangs. She addressed us by our surnames (preceded by "Mister" or "Miss") in the authoritative, low-pitched voice of an elocutionist. Everyone regarded her as a grandmotherly figure, and because she'd been teaching for decades, she'd taught several of our other teachers.

Whenever we presented a note written in her perfect cursive, begging their pardon to miss class for a rehearsal or arrive late, the teachers always excused us. A note from Ms. Seals meant we were doing something worthwhile and civilizing—algebra, typing and world history could wait.

It's likely Ms. Seals reminded me of Price. Her sound and carriage were Black but refined by something I found nonnative to the thoroughly Black landscape of my life.

Choir was its own universe. We had slang and signifiers like any other clique, but we could also harmonize—breathing, swelling and articulating as one. This fierceness made us an obnoxious, raucous and insufferable bunch. You couldn't tell us nothing. We could weaponize a Bach chorale. It was glorious.

Choir gave me cover, a sense of belonging in an otherwise cruel high school world. It's also where I first encountered the singing fundamentals my classmates had already learned in the Black church. I was Catholic, and music for Mass included organ playing, chanting and the white priests' off-key singing.

I learned to harmonize, blend with other singers, produce clear vowels and sing through the *passaggi* (the *passageways* or breaks between the voice's lower, middle and upper ranges). This was my entree into bel canto ("beautiful singing"), the storied Italian method characterized by evenness of tone, clarity and agility.

The famed Italian singing teacher Francesco Lamperti proclaimed, "Chi sa respirare . . . saprá ben cantare" ("One who breathes well, sings well"). Singers must master breath. Without it, there's no voice.

At inhalation, the rib cage, abdomen and back enlarge to create a vacuum that rushes oxygen into the lungs. With their sternums held unnaturally erect, singers ride upon a cushion of breath. (Hence, the caricature of the ballooning and barrel-chested opera singer.) The exhaled air passes through the vocal folds to produce the sound we call singing.

Junior year, the codirectors of Youth Opera Theatre at Xavier University took me to audition for Leon Baptiste, a respected and long-retired Black tenor and teacher. After hearing me sing the aria "Vecchia zimarra" (from *La Boheme*), he accepted me as a student.

He started me with pieces from the G. Schirmer edition of *Twenty-Four Italian Songs & Arias of the 17th and 18th Centuries*, workhorses for teaching phrasing, breath control and the basis of all classical technique: vowels. Italian is indispensable for learning to produce *pure* vowels.

Southerners—as if inebriated by the gaping languor of our own vowels—echo the sound of our forebears, the British. Our elongated vowels lend themselves to operatic sound. Think Blanche in *The Golden Girls*. Vowels pulled like taffy.

Pure vowels root the singing voice more deeply within the body, automatically amplifying its volume and beauty. This is true for anyone, but particularly for Americans, who find themselves suddenly *disclosing* more voice than they thought possible.

For a dispossessed gay Black kid like me, this was how I came to understand the voice as *metaphor*—something precious to seek out, excavate, polish and display. Throat already dilated by the patois of New Orleans, mine was a treasure to be heard, infinitely exponential and *loud*.

BEL CANTO

(During the first six months of his vocal study, famed tenor Luciano Pavarotti was only allowed to vocalize, or sing, vowels. *Ah*, *Ee* and *Ooh* are especially difficult.)

Ah

Most maritime of all
Uvula vaulted
gorged & glistening

Tide arrived
as sound

Tongue resting in the cradle
dumb

Ee

Tongue thinned
slightly risen
to palate

Soft jaw

Raised curtain of lip
to teeth

Such movement
perfumes each cheek
burnishes bone

Ooh

Dim
the lips

Let
a slender leg of breath
have its way
through chambers:

Apart from Black people (who speak with more depthful sonority than most in this republic), Americans often relegate their voice to the nasal passages, where it flattens into a tinny, unmelodious sound. These voices emerge from bodies yet sound *dis*embodied. What their sound lacks in tonal beauty, nuance and moral authority, they make up for through volume, repetition, conviction.

To practice, I found an old upright for $150 in the *Times Picayune*. Cheap as it was, Willie still shit on it. "Don't ask me for nothing else, you hear?" We moved it out of an old white woman's Uptown house, overrun with cats. The only place to put it was my bedroom, where I teared up and sneezed for days.

Soon it was covered with music scores and photocopies of scores graffitied with pencil markings to accelerate or accent, decrescendo or breathe, to soften a consonant or sharpen its bone.

Wedged between the drafty window and floor heater, in time, its keys stuck and hammers failed. But in the wake of the levee breach of Katrina, it remained sentinel, the most imposing and essential furniture of my sky-blue bedroom.

UPRIGHT
New Orleans, 2006

for Jake Adam York

My piano stood firm
even as water took the linoleum
& the long gone rose again
to cadence

I played when the levees held back
the brine
before the storm-snapped hammers

I played through the savagery
of high school
before these octaves were fibrous
with mold

If only the dark pearled ebony
If only
If only the spindles

Bring the yellow teeth & hard
bench
the syllables descending
in the left hand

like this

I still laugh about its stint as the hidden repository for my sacred, teenage sacrament.

THE ACTION

It was from the bottom of my upright piano
behind the panel beneath the keyboard
that I drew my deepest adolescent breaths
where I hid gay porn in the late '80s
practicing my scales & gospel chords above *Hung*
& *Blue Boy*
Freshmen & *Inches*

Men inside my piano
hammers
sweetening the wood

My fingers & wrists positioning
elbows drawn in
my foot pumping the pedal
sounding & sounding
until it rose to art

Dog-eared pages that summoned my quiver
& shameless music
where I binged on youth in my messy bedsheets

the muscle memory of how to grow up
a brown instrument with hidden stables
for my ever-bruising unbreakable stallions

The voice I had then was a composite produced amid repression and resignation, but also through the radiant stamina of Momma and Aunt Trina, teachers and the various castes of my all-Black community. It was *irreducible*. They claimed my voice, its lineage and elemental belonging—even if it sounded "proper" like that "opera music."

Singled out and praised for my voice. Solace in the blight. Because I could abide in Price and worship not just the god-object of her voice, but what it enacted inside and materialized around me.

Solace because I'd never possess such immensity, and that, thankfully, provided a measure and contour of my otherwise half-lit and indiscernible self.

Despite acceptances from Peabody Conservatory and my first choice, Oberlin, after the head of the voice department called to reassure Mr. Baptiste ("We're a small school. Kevin can receive a lot of personal attention here"), the scholarships and aid from what had been a "safety school" decided it: I would attend Vanderbilt's Blair School of Music.

Like Price, my teachers, family and community had nestled me inside a tangible Black continuum. I lived close to the materials, the source. I felt it.

When I left New Orleans and arrived at Vanderbilt, the major forms and figures of the source immediately became minor or absent. But Ms. Seals and Mr. Baptiste had warned me:

> *Don't let them change your voice. It's a naturally dark sound. Like Price.*

Referred to in the third person, the voice is entirely dependent on a human body for its production, the instrument indivisible from the singer. To oversee the raising and care of the voice goes beyond the ordinary responsibilities of any music teacher. Not only that, voice teachers face a hazard unique to them, one their instrumental peers needn't ever worry about: they can *ruin* an instrument.

Music students are typically in close quarters, but Blair was unusually small. (Including me, there were only 31 freshmen and probably no more than 120 students total in my four years there.) The customary theorizing and debating ideas among college undergrads is, at a school of music, the domain of composition and history majors. Only they are truly free to question, challenge and renounce.

Performance majors are *apprentices*, selected by audition, and assigned to teachers based on that audition. Of course, matching teachers with students involves rules and traditions driven by hierarchy and politics.

A student oboist may apply solely to study with the professor who is the principal oboist in the local orchestra, and the cello faculty may fight over the winner of a regional concerto competition.

These pairings are highly subjective and biased, but instrumentalists must exhibit technical facility to assure their prospective teachers of an aptitude for mastering an instrument and its repertoire. The voice is another thing altogether.

Because the voice can mature more slowly and unpredictably than other instruments, in an audition, teachers tend to rely less on technical proficiency and home in on other predictive indicators such as timbre (color), vibrato, control, consistency, range, size and stamina. Doing so gives voice teachers great latitude and subjective cover, and final studio assignments (and reassignments) can often be inscrutable to students.

An audition may convince one teacher of great potential, with them welcoming the student into their studio. Another may hear a "derivative" sound unworthy of their time. A third may want to take on the student after a couple of years, once the voice has begun "settling," "smoothing out" or "better negotiating" this or that so its *real quality* can emerge. Vast sensibilities shape how voice teachers hear or purport to hear.

"Schools" of singing, which include national, technical and sonic lineages and pedigrees, too, may influence conclusions about a student's suitability. And period preferences such as Baroque, Classical, Modern may compete with devotions to certain eras or stylistic affectations—complete with their own unique constellations of operatic stars known for *that* sound, approach or interpretation.

Voice teachers must coax sound from young people whose bodies lurch and stall from late adolescence into young adulthood. It's a complicated time for any teacher-student relationship—but one distinction sets the journey of a voice teacher and their student apart from all others: the sheer carnality, its demands of physical intimacy.

Voice teachers often touch their students' bodies or have them touch theirs: to model breathing, to ascertain if the back remains engaged during the long phrase, the shoulders relaxed, the knees unlocked, the ribs aloft.

While it's given that the voice and the singer are physically indivisible, it's also vital that they're addressed *separately* and rendered *divisible*— mostly for the sake of the student's confidence, self-esteem and well-being.

I tried to keep Ms. Seals and Mr. Baptiste's admonition ("Don't let them change your voice") as lodestar. I tried to protect my "naturally dark sound"—that one thing I thought could be taken away and *trained out* of me by my teachers—all white—who constantly instructed me not to "cover" and "manufacture" something "darker," but to "thin" and "brighten" the sound.

Of the countless recordings my professors played in class or assigned for listening tests, none featured a Black singer, unless it was for a unit on Black music or, as that time in German Diction, when Nat King Cole's rendition of "O Tannenbaum" served as cautionary tale.

LOOSE ASSEMBLAGE OF THAT
UNMOORED STUDENT SELF

music history
chapter on the blues
lone black me
ashamed it took
such holler
such buck in me
the bars in me

Black and closeted, I didn't dare draw attention to myself at a school so overrun with white conservatives and Christians. While other students were excitedly exploring their sexuality, I was praying for *deliverance* from my own. Singing was my only sensual expression.

Of course, my teachers couldn't have known how desperate I was to convey just some of the heat of my dark diva interior.

> *White Americans seem to feel that happy songs are happy and sad songs are sad, and that, God help us, is exactly the way most white Americans sing them—sounding, in both cases, so helplessly, defenselessly fatuous that one dare not speculate on the temperature of the deep freeze from which issue their brave and sexless little voices.*
>
> James Baldwin

Eventually, I obliged and contracted (as I'd done in grade school), this time relinquishing the right to be heard with such a dark and heavy voice. Before long, I began to have chronic vocal problems that stemmed from an increasing inability to manage the breath.

Chi sa respirare . . . saprá ben cantare.

Before telling me I had "more to offer and more to gain" than anyone in Intro to Shakespeare, Dr. Cook compared her white-girl journey—from Wewoka, Oklahoma, to a tenured professorship at Vanderbilt and international renown as a Shakespeare scholar—with my freshman arrival.

After that, no professor ever made me feel welcome—at least, went out of their way to show me that they saw me. Instead, they routinely ignored me, were contemptuous, condescending or treated me as an intruder. All were unfailingly successful in relaying their exasperation in trying to *remediate* me.

The price I paid for that (in tens of thousands in student loans too) was high: estrangement not only from the confidence and expectation to become better, but from my right to their paid service.

Price's voice accomplished itself over and over. She commanded the blistering melodies of Verdi, the unyielding bravura of Mozart and the pyrotechnics of Strauss and Puccini—with the same voice that set the standard for interpretations of Negro spirituals and American art songs.

Listening to Price's earliest recordings (keeping in mind that her teacher Florence Page Kimball said that she'd arrived at Juilliard already possessing a "dark molasses sound"), I wonder how much of her definitive dark sound had been encouraged and groomed in New York.

Price's first and most lasting inspiration was Marian Anderson. When she was nine years old, she saw Anderson perform in recital in Jackson, Mississippi. The darkness of Anderson's voice, one that, like Price's, emerged from the Black church, surely reinforced the expectation of a racialized sound.

Black sopranos and mezzo-sopranos following Price in the 1960s (including Martina Arroyo, Grace Bumbry and Shirley Verrett) couldn't have resisted her influence or the *expectation* of a Black sound. All were critically praised for their dark timbres, and all had begun singing in the Black church.

When Rudolf Bing offered her a Met debut as Aida, Price said no. She felt she'd accrued enough professional capital to *defy* those who insisted on limiting her to the role of a Black singer or character. Of course, she hadn't always done this. The troubling racial vehicles of *Porgy and Bess* and *Four Saints in Three Acts* launched her career. Whatever her reasons, before turning down Bing's invitation, she'd acquiesced to white expectation: Black sound—exotic and ghettoized—in its proper place. Those were the terms, the demands.

Had Mr. Baptiste instilled in me the sound of a bygone era? Is that what my voice professors at Blair tried to rid me of? Not my "naturally dark sound" but a dated, racialized affect?

acousmatic blackness: that which signifies—
earnest or otherwise—a particular sound

emancipated or emaciated (depending on one's
discriminating faculties)—

drawn from coon songs field hollers vaudeville
work songs ring shouts spirituals—

in this case *notatable* and *singable*
by gowned recitalists

in the bends of pianos
but often bulging through

the delicate skins of European art song
and the aria

The height or breadth of the forehead, the size of the cranium, the prominence of the occipital bone, the dimensions of the mandible, and the length and height of the nose bridge do not determine resonance. Contemporary speculation that a large nose ought to give an indication of greater resonance is not surprising, inasmuch as that notion was generally held by some teachers of the eighteenth and nineteenth centuries, who refused to accept singers who lacked large noses.

Richard Miller, *Solutions for Singers:*
Tools for Performers and Teachers

Contemporary vocal scientists agree there are **no morphological differences that indicate race**. *Therefore, there should be* **no timbral differences based on race. However . . . people do hear racially-based timbral differences**. *I argue that such differences are based on the flexibility and possibility of the instrument, and the* **choices made** *as to which aspects of an individual vocal timbre to bring forward. Thus expressive* **limitations** *are the results* **of choice of use** *rather than of* **physical premises**.

Vocal sound is shaped by the size and shape of the vocal tract and the mouth cavity—both modified by the singer's **manipulation**.

Nina Sun Eidsheim, "Voice as a Technology
of Selfhood: Towards an Analysis of
Racialized Timbre and Vocal Performance"

chiaroscuro: the quality a singer trained in bel canto aspires to produce by simultaneously summoning a brilliant sonance (*squillo*) and a darker sonance (*scurro*)

The accomplished bel canto singer synthesizes this light-darkness to achieve a depth and warmth unrivaled in other schools of singing.

A CASE *FOR* AND *AGAINST* BLACK SOUND

1

held open—say
by the long-dead

a surge tracing somehow
—a now

a human noise
an instrument eye—

part feature
part flattened

why?

the blood
carved open—say

willing away the drying
black clay

the blood
carved open—say

by an instrument eye
willing away—somehow

the matter
of the black clay

2

a why?
barreling through—say

3

an *away*
instrument

If you take Jessye Norman or Leontyne Price or somebody
like that: they do opera. And so, that's not really Black
music.

You notice the absences later   (Leontyne

                      Paul Robeson

because the seven minutes of this acclaimed film

                      Katherine Dunham

transfix so thoroughly

                      Alvin Ailey)

without a nod to white-willed form
provenance walled, perfumed
with leisure

       And if you know opera well enough you could probably
       make the case that they bring a Black sensibility to what
       they're doing.

minor thirds
of the body
summed

erry bone picked
                clean
erry joint
                bent

erry note
the capacity

        to blue

> *But fundamentally that form evolved over several hundred years of the pressure of the people who sort of formulated it to articulate certain sorts of—I guess you could say—existential circumstances.*

Forms shadowed by distinct
relationship
to stereotype phenotype
not necessarily *genotype*

> *In other words, it's an instrument that evolved under the pressure of articulating certain kinds of things. So even if a person of African descent—a Leontyne Price let's say for example—is singing* Aida, *which is actually even about Africans, right—that still doesn't make it African or Black music.*

Melanin adjusts.
(The melanated—not always)

Yet there are skinfolk
not so far gone or future
to sound without that one-drop
confessing

      Leontyne

Like somewhere in New Orleans
Doreen throws back her head to blow

presses keys & becomes sound
she *can* control

      Leontyne

The clarinet is not her body
but a stand-in

seizing
the unsayable

      Leontyne

There can be no remission of sins
without blood
or its sound

after Arthur Jafa at Berkeley Art Museum and Pacific Film Archive, discussing his film Love Is the Message, the Message Is Death, *December 10, 2018*

PERFORMANCE

monster (n.): from the Latin *monere*, "to remind, bring to (one's) recollection, tell (of); admonish, advise, warn, instruct, teach."

⫴⫴ **Leontyne Price, soprano**

(in order of appearance)

David Garvey, pianist
Mrs. William Jordan Rapp, concerned citizen
Samuel Barber, composer
Simone Leigh, artist
Dorothy Dandridge, film star
Marian Anderson, contralto
Grace Bumbry, soprano
Eartha Kitt, singer and actor
James Baldwin, writer
George B. Price, brigadier general,
brother of Leontyne Price
Ruth Bader Ginsburg, Supreme Court justice
Beverly Sills, soprano
Alvin Ailey, dancer and choreographer
FBI agents
Members of the press

America,
I couldn't have sounded like this
anywhere else

Grooves cut down to bone
a terror

                    a reprieve

I constitute an order
through sound men imagine
but could never make

What you hear
is an *other* matter yes
technique as ladder

but already
the summit
of my sound

Seldom do people ask how it feels
to be on fire and feed it

Stand there a valve
a filter a veil

and contain what should bust me
wide open

as I swim the depths
breath imperceptible

No one read palms
worked roots
Some prayed
Some didn't
Mostly it was luck and I knew
not to push it
but to nail myself
to only this
is what I mean
mark myself
before anyone else could

Like my brigadier general brother
      I enlisted to serve

When country calls, I hammer
      land that I love

I drill
      my home, sweet home

This Old Girl still got good aim
      and bullets to fire

But the target has got to be
      mine

Affirmative action requirements under Title VI and VII are said repeatedly "not to require the hiring of any unqualified individuals" . . . If I can't get Leontyne Price to sing a concert I have scheduled, I may have to settle for Erma Glatt. La Glatt has a pretty good voice, but not as good as Price. Is she unqualified? Not really—she has sung other concerts with modest success. But she is just not as good as Price. Any system that coerces me to hire her in preference to Price, because of her race, degrades the quality of my product and discriminates on racial grounds against Price.

Antonin Scalia

⑊⑊ Self-Portrait

As icon
As inkblot
As race mule

UNITED STATES GOVERNMENT

TO: DIRECTOR, FBI   DATE: MAY 29, 1952
FROM: FIELD AGENT
RE: LEONTYNE PRICE

The SUBJECT starred in performances of
composer VIRGIL THOMSON'S opera "Four Saints
in Three Acts" tonight and last night to
enthusiastic audiences. The State Department
financed the adaptation, as well as the
entire festival, and Festival Secretary,
composer NICOLAS NABOKOV, a Soviet émigré and
United States citizen, and first cousin of
noted novelist VLADIMIR NABOKOV, also a Soviet
émigré and United States citizen, helped
convince PRICE to participate. This cast of
negroes should forestall criticisms of the
negro problem. Deceased sex deviant GERTRUDE
STEIN wrote the libretto, and THOMSON, also a
sex deviant, was in attendance.

PRICE is soon to marry singer WILLIAM
WARFIELD, who appears in last year's MGM
remake of "Showboat" as the character who
sings "Ole Man River," but omits the lyrics,
"Niggers all work on de Mississippi, Niggers
all work while de white folks play," which
were sung by known Negro Communist PAUL
ROBESON in the 1936 Universal Pictures
version. The Security Index Card concerning
the subject is being maintained.

Her seduction reaches standing room
with nothing lost in the velocity of her tide

I want to do that but like this:
I will undress *them*

after Salome *with soprano Ljuba Welitsch,
the Metropolitan Opera House, 1949*

I think my people are right—we are right because, for one reason, we are finally prepared. No group at all, minority or not, no matter what color they are, can actually be strong if they are not prepared . . . Well, the blood of the black man is in the soil of this country. But this time there is no way out.

Leontyne Price

Even when I can't see her face
I know—

Her breath or the shaping
of the phrase

The aperture of her arms
her satellite hands

Keys shimmering leaves
as we ride

David Garvey (March 13, 1922–February 14, 1995) was
Price's exclusive accompanist from 1955 until his death.

Self-Portrait as Cover

My Kevlar composure
belies the real threat

Three hours from Laurel
where Meredith flew

took fire registering
for class in '62

I integrated St. Paul's
in '63

First time ever in Laurel
2,000 came for me

The murders at 16th Street
Three hours from Laurel some casings

at my feet

In '55 I was Tosca on TV
the year Ms. Parks kept her seat

All these years later
too few casings

at my feet

My Kevlar composure
belies my exposure

Self-Portrait as Folktale of the Senses

The Soprano knew her best chance was to have Someone *hear* her. Yet with Everyone's *sight* to contend with, she had to perform the inherited roles of those who looked as she did. It was advised that those roles could *touch* Everyone or, at least, Someone, in different ways and for different reasons. Someone said her voice wasn't to their *taste*. Someone said her being there—in that costume, in that role, on that stage with her hand in his hand—was bad *taste*. She was uppity and they could *smell* it. The Soprano had good sense but couldn't bear trying to *touch* Everyone. She wasn't to Everyone's *taste*. She could *smell* it. But despite Everyone, she stuck to her own senses. Someone might understand this. But it's certain Everyone won't.

⫘ The Movement

Which?

Virgil Thomson had chosen Harlem Negroes because of their diction. White singers, he feared, would act foolish and self-conscious chanting such lines as "Let Lucy Lily Lily Lucy Lucy let Lucy Lucy Lily Lily Lily Lily Lily let Lily Lucy Lucy let Lily. Let Lucy Lily" . . . *The Negroes sang them as fervently as though the silly words had a saintly meaning* . . .

Time

Its spell was to be found in the natural talent of Negroes for playing seriously like a lot of children . . . *They knelt and rolled their eyes toward stage heaven, genuflected, saint before saint with the deepest gravity, and sang their nonsense syllables with as much faith and devotion as they might have sung, "It's me, Lord, standin' in the need of prayer"* . . . *Maybe it was meant to be a burlesque on "grand opera." If so, it is a gorgeous success.*

W. J. Henderson

Price presented with her Donna Anna the same obtrusive incongruity as previously with her Leonora in Il Trovatore *and her Pamina in* The Magic Flute *but not with her* Aida: *When I look at what is happening on a stage, my imagination still cannot accommodate itself to a black in the role of a white.*

Bernard H. Haggin

Mrs. Alexander Chisholm talks. She is accustomed to audiences. James Price sits back in his seat, looks over his right shoulder at her, listens. Mrs. Chisholm leans over the back of Kate Price's seat, her right arm resting across the top. Kate Price is not sitting back in her seat like her husband. She cannot. She turns her body left toward Mrs. Chisholm, looks into her face. Mrs. Chisholm looks down, talks. She is accustomed to looking elsewhere while others study her face to discern what she means. Kate Price looks like she wants Mrs. Chisholm to stop talking and get off her seat so she can sit back. Alfred Eisenstaedt is on assignment for *Time* magazine and this evening takes many photographs before and after this one. None depict Kate Price slapping Mrs. Chisholm because this night means so much to so many.

after a photograph by Alfred Eisenstaedt, January 27, 1961

~~acousmatic~~ blackness: a franchise one simply can't revise

Let us not mis-use our arts for propaganda
in the communist manner

this casting of a negress
without excuse

vis-à-vis white men
in such necessarily romantic scenes

is misguided
offensive

this isn't *Aida*

no objection to Miss Price personally that
excellent voice

after letter to the president of NBC from
Mrs. William Jordan Rapp, 1955

It's convenient to make me
a stowaway to my sound

because I look as I do
not because of where I'm from

A sound can come
from anywhere

I've never been to Laurel
and likely never will

I only know Leontyne
and the scythe of her sound

Even on radio—
My god!

Mississippi wouldn't air
her *Tosca* on NBC

That was 1955
but they've come so far

She's a credit to their movement
diplomat to the whole world

My muse my
Cleopatra

※

Men like me wish
we had her sound

the clearing it makes
to be unhidden

possessed by sound that began
before a mother made it

hanging laundry no
before the cushion of amniotic fluid

the congregation of a girl raptured by sound
she too would make

for men who scratch out notes
first

to build a throat
and then

to hold its breath
when this soprano sings

Samuel Barber (March 9, 1910–January 23, 1981), one of the most celebrated composers of the twentieth century, began writing for Price in 1953 with the debut of *Hermit Songs*. Chosen to compose the opera *Antony and Cleopatra* for the opening of the new Metropolitan Opera House at Lincoln Center in 1966, he wrote the role of Cleopatra for Price.

Self-Portrait as Skirted Black Lady

Ankles crossed
Angled knees
Held tight
Smile shellacked
Summary symbol
Circumspect

Amnesiac

ARRANGEMENT OF LEIGH/LEE

by relating her to my own body
her edges and presence in space

my hand figures / the skirt form

needing a handle
to lift

the jug of her body / to my body's

mouth
drink her down

to creolize / is no loophole no

retreat
the crawlspace of her

to look out from / is not a fiction

she / we
the archive

Simone Leigh (born 1967) is an artist who works in various
media such as sculpture and is widely known for her
explorations of Black female subjectivity.

Anybody would want to lip-synch to you
I know they asked, and you couldn't
Marilyn's wonderful
(her husband's a Negro, you know)
I study her mouth to know what to do
But with you, I would've felt it

I missed that honor

When do we expect they'll let us
all the way in?
With your voice, we could've shown them
what they're missing
Wouldn't we have been quite
a woman?

Dorothy Dandridge (November 9, 1922–September 8,
1965) was a film and theater actress, singer and dancer. She
portrayed the title character in the 1954 movie *Carmen Jones*,
an adaptation of the 1943 Broadway musical of the same
name. In this version, Carmen is a Black woman working in a
parachute factory in North Carolina during World War II.

Captive,
      pass through
            us Aida
            us Ulrica
            us Bess
   us princess
   us seer
   us shore
            us slave
            us Negress
            us addict
   scale us

Marian

   us lengths

Leontyne

   lap up
   us milk
   stride
   us stride

   wait out
   us spasms
   smother
   us phantoms

acousmatic blackness: widely understood as *Negraoke*

Catfish Row is home
for now

Halfway right about the Negro situation
and every night I play midwife

until it bears more
of a family resemblance

It's all we've got and not
all bad

But *easy*?
Never easy

Being Bess was already half of me . . . I mean, most of me anyway.

Leontyne Price

Bess, we let loose
made white lies
into a lullaby

Hands on hips
high-heeled and hot-combed
you hid the bruises from me

so I could just sing

I never forgot you
or forgave you all
that applause

Catfish Row still
has my number
no matter Cleopatra

No matter the crown
you'll never wear

⫼⫿ That final high G

Good-bye, Porgy! Good-bye——————!

got me *Tosca*

It's not even *that*

high

but it's more

than the coordinates

It's the fade

to black

There were things that happened to my voice that should not have happened.

Marian Anderson

First time I mixed the witch's brew
they applauded *before* I sang

Brown vs. Board, now me
and soon your Tosca on NBC

Eight times I mixed the witch's brew
and *knew* it came too late

Have a fortune-teller's sight, dear
tighten your trill around their throats

Suffocate them all
with all your notes

Marian Anderson (February 27, 1897–April 8, 1993) was an
American singer who, denied use of Constitution Hall by
the Daughters of the American Revolution to sing before an
integrated audience, received help from Eleanor Roosevelt,
who arranged a performance on the steps of the Lincoln
Memorial on April 9, 1939. On January 7, 1955, Anderson
became the first Black singer at the Metropolitan Opera.

UNITED STATES GOVERNMENT

TO: DIRECTOR, FBI   DATE: FEBRUARY 28, 1965

FROM: FIELD AGENT

RE: LEONTYNE PRICE

Famous singer LEONTYNE PRICE made her
CARNEGIE HALL DEBUT tonight. Sang two songs
by female Negro composer MARGARET BONDS who
she called "a very good friend of mine" before
singing "Lord, I Just Can't Keep from Crying
Sometimes" and "He's Got the Whole World in
His Hands." BONDS is a long-time associate and
close friend of famous Negro poet LANGSTON
HUGHES, a known homosexual, who has ties to
Communist-related groups going back to at
least 1932 when he traveled to the Soviet
Union with 22 other negros to act in a film.
Then in 1933, he was the principal speaker
at a luncheon at the Imperial Hotel in Tokyo
where he predicted a time would come when all
the colored races would join in subjugating
whites. This "alleged" poet remains a
Communist. Although his more recent writings
are less boldly subversive, see 3/13/41 L.A.
File 100-1960 to read his poem "Goodbye
Christ." This information is furnished for
whatever value it may possess.

I am Aida in many senses . . . Aida was royalty.

Leontyne Price

This Laurel girl to fill in
for a sick Aida

Here I am skin-assured
to throttle through

Never been a time I haven't
been ready

Had to wait for this
for them

to catch up

San Francisco Opera, 1957

Aida

you cannot make
a willow
out of an oak
this maidservant held close
to break
she summons the tributaries
into her
she chooses
breathlessness

I know that already I have made the choice I want to make. But I'm in my mid-thirties, and I'm a little bit too young to be quite so preoccupied and narrow-minded about what I am doing. I think I would like to, at sixty or let's say fifty, not be so preoccupied with whether my high C is going to come out or not, but really try to do something for somebody else . . . to be available for things that may help people.

Leontyne Price

Lenny asked for "Somewhere"
and that settled it

We'd lost I don't know
how many

Liz stuck by Rock
and raised millions

Us Cleopatras know *we hate*
what we often fear

Sam, Virgil, Gian Carlo
pool parties at Capricorn

Will and his
bathroom "mix-ups"

Look at who we've lost
Look at who we haven't

after the AIDS benefit concert "Music for Life"
Carnegie Hall, November 8, 1987

1

On the summer streets of Vienna like anywhere else
you acknowledged other Black people
That's how I met Hugh in '59
when he invited me to meet her

Nobody knew who I was then

2

Sol took me backstage after the Met *Trovatore*
and she reminded me we'd met
even offered to send her car to my hotel
so I wouldn't have to wait

I aspired to become gracious
like that
especially to us

3

I came behind her at the Met in '65 and it was still bad
the dressers wigmakers the makeup people
some of the other singers

—until they heard you
but not always not everyone
This gilded world is no different

We'd turned down those dinner-as-served roles
and waited to go
full gallop

4

Years later we roared in the listening room
amazed with our blend in the boudoir scene

You, *Prima Donna Assoluta*
Me, *Black Venus*

5

I admired her to no end
I didn't care *what* she did

She could've picked at the grass!

That voice excused
everything

Grace Bumbry (born January 4, 1937), acclaimed American
opera singer, was, in 1961, the first Black singer to perform at
the Bayreuth Festival.

｜｜｜｜｜ For a girl of nine
white satin is dream enough

But you in the curve
of the black grand

billowing from the altar
twisting into me as prophecy

2

Resurrection Sunday, 1939
with Lincoln as your plinth

the daughters who said no
to sisterhood

the 75,000 you look out upon
and those you reach though radio

like me
you enunciate our dignity

God and Mrs. Roosevelt turned you loose
You are mighty among us, Miss Anderson

I am only 12 but I know

3

Once in a hundred years
is faulty math, Maestro Toscanini

You measured against time
as the clay-footed usually do

We aren't so narrow
We aren't so arrogant

4

When I was worn down
by what passed for decency
when I was recognized or not
Imprimatur, you

5

Among the pastel taffeta
the smiles pulled tight across
these white-woman faces: us

This does not correct itself
so we must make a show of it
together

6

Even my gown
is black

Daughters of the American Revolution,
91st Continental Congress, April 20, 1982

I never talk about difficulties. Once the success is there, it's not only boring, it is exasperating.

Leontyne Price

notes on exile

history accumulates in Black voice

imagine the sound withheld

in viselike

decorum

even at full cry to serve the flat form

her labor disorients

etherealizes their compulsion

distracts from fugitive sound

       the charismata of the congregation
       decides your blue your blue is blood sound, sister

       dry bones
       should rise

꧁꧂ Dear, this wasn't no Chitlin' Circuit
not Ella's or Lena's crowd

This was box seats passed
from one generation

of Vanderbilts Carnegies Astors and Guggenheims
to the next

Dynasties with ledgers and holdings:
Conquerors

I wasn't singing some slave strain
collected with asterisked note

>   *This is an approximation*
>   *because the Negro never*

>   *sang it the same or kept*
>   *to key or rhythm*

I mastered the fixed notes
of Mozart Puccini Verdi and Strauss

I had to kill their phantoms with poise
and a swallowing silence

Do you hear?
I had to clear

my
throat

LP

testing 1-2
needle / narcotic

testing 3-4
diagnostic / deposit

at the spine

withdrawal:

I Mind My Own
                Business

Take   My   Time
To Clean

        The Carcass

                Force

        A Pause

        A Sonic
        Restitution

And Her

Every Cell

Sings

Eartha Kitt (January 17, 1927–December 25, 2008) was a
singer, actor, dancer and activist.

SCENARIO
VISIT OF HIS HOLINESS JOHN PAUL II
Saturday, October 6, 1979

3:45 P.M.   THE PRESIDENT, MRS. CARTER
and His Holiness

John Paul II escorted to Blue Room and
proceed out to balcony to descend West
Staircase to Speaker's platform.

Leontyne Price sings "The Lord's Prayer"
by Malotte.

I	just	love	the	sound	of	my	own
				voice			
I	just	love	the	sound	of	my	own
				voice			
I	just	love	the	sound	of	my	own
				voice			
I	just	love	the	sound	of	my	own
				voice			
I	just	love	the	sound	of	my	own
				voice			
I	just	love	the	sound	of	my	own
				voice			
I	just	love	the	sound	of	my	own
				voice			

4:25 P.M.   At the conclusion of walk, THE PRESIDENT and
MRS. CARTER and His Holiness John Paul II
go to the West Balcony stairs.

As they ascend stairway, Leontyne Price
sings "America the Beautiful."

I	just	love	the	sound	of	my	own
				voice			
I	just	love	the	sound	of	my	own
				voice			
I	just	love	the	sound	of	my	own
				voice			
I	just	love	the	sound	of	my	own
				voice			
I	just	love	the	sound	of	my	own
				voice			
I	just	love	the	sound	of	my	own
				voice			
I	just	love	the	sound	of	my	own
				voice			

JAMES BALDWIN AND R. H. DARDEN IN CONVERSATION, 1968

JB: All black Americans are treated like niggers—
Sammy Davis Jr. to my mother.

RHD: You still feel yourself treated in that fashion—

JB: As long as my brothers—and I have
four brothers and five sisters—and my mother is
and she's alive—and many, many more people
than that are treated as they are. My being in the
Beverly Hills Hotel has nothing to do with it.

RHD: Uh, speaking in the generality, perhaps not—

JB: I'm not speaking in the generality, I'm
talking about my family.

RHD: But there are such dramatic exceptions, Mr.
Baldwin, yourself being one—

JB: There are no exceptions—

RHD: Leontyne Price?

JB: There are no exceptions—

RHD: No exceptions?

JB: No.

RHD: You're saying, in effect then, that as long as black
Americans on the street and you on the street—

JB: If they don't know that she's Leontyne
Price, she still can't get a taxi.

RHD: In New York?

JB: In New York, in the North. I won't talk about the South.

✳

Even with her long Mississippi vowels. Even centered by the royal shade of her middle name, the immaculate virtue of her first:

Miss Mary Violet Leontyne Price, your daughter.

Of the South.

Even with her outdoing everybody in an art form that you have turned into another *occasion to hallucinate* the absolute subjugation of anybody *not* white—all while being sung to lavishly—you would deny her—have denied her. That voice happening right before us.

From her *black* throat.

How, then, can I explain anything to you about this republic? About *you*, my countrymen, who can't seem to get enough of my people hemorrhaging the blues and jazz and R&B and rock & roll?

And, now, you can't get enough of her. If you close your eyes, you can almost imagine her being white, can't you? The American Dream: eyes shut or averted. Or so wide in terror that—no matter the song-stirred evidence that we are kin—you refuse to defect and renounce the Heritage that will doom us all.

(And to think, in three days of this interview, Dr. King will be killed. But we can't unhear him. Not you, not me. Not the junior high school students who he told just months ago:

> *If it falls your lot to be a street sweeper, sweep streets*
> *like Michelangelo painted pictures, sweep streets like*
> *Beethoven composed music, sweep streets like Leontyne*
> *Price sings before the Metropolitan Opera.*)

They had nothing on my sister
they could use
to silence her

But they could make things
difficult
shall we say

That's where I came in
to take measures
she couldn't

✻

I fought in Vietnam
and for the Memorial
wound in the earth

Upright a black
stone wall polished
to see our faces
and name the costs

I fought for Lee
upright a black
stone wall smoked
with the named
and unnamed
the difference that stares
and staves

George B. Price (born August 29, 1929), retired army
brigadier general and Price's brother, became her manager in
1984.

Astride a white stallion
she saves her fella from the rope
a gambling woman with a gun

Price was perfect, you see
for *Fanciulla* to have teeth
and for *Butterfly*

To flutter your lashes
and withhold your reserves
To make that choice

Yes, to the hand of aces in the garter
Yes, to the fair maiden
who leaves nothing in her wake

At Arlington
send me on the chariot
of *that* woman-voice

Ruth Bader Ginsburg (March 15, 1933–September 18, 2020)
was an associate justice of the Supreme Court of the United
States from 1993 until her death.

All token Blacks have the same experience. I have been pointed at as a solution to things that have not yet begun to be solved, because pointing at us token Blacks eases consciences of millions, and this is dreadfully wrong.

Leontyne Price

Self-Portrait in February

Exhumed—
the turban confuses
the youngins
while the seniors nod
a reflexive *amen* that she sang high notes
for presidents
and how that must've been hard
to make the race proud
and the presidents too
back when there was so little
Black history

Other People's Problems

Token. Black.

Achievement has no color

That space given to me

by my country

the Man Upstairs

I don't mean *en couleur*

It was broader than that

always was

Now get on with it

⑈⑈⑈ On Technique

for the voice to arrive indigenous verb

to herd
transmit

shimmy
jackknife

tremble
elate

exhaust
tilt

hold
trigger

ravage
shade, yes

slay, yes
signal yes yes

torque this form
into a runaway sound
(they hear
what comforts
never
insurrection)
the haunting bray
of a bejeweled and disobedient
mule

Deposits *on* the sound?
Or is the sound
the deposit?

They bind to my voice
follow its registers
forget they wouldn't follow me

any
    other
        way

These young people at the counters
the dogs and hoses
that baby boy Emmett

Dr. King speaks the King's English
can get a congregation up on their feet
but they're the proverbial choir, lambs

I'm talking here
      about
      wolves

If NASA were serious
they'd beam Lee's voice through space
to make contact
The Martians would arrive
cure for cancer in hand
proofs for every theorem
if they could simply stand
in her vibration

If we were serious
after the triumphant final aria
when she's just another lady eyeing
something through a store window
we'd look at her, smile
open the door and invite her in
call her *ma'am*

Beverly Sills (May 25, 1929–July 2, 2007) was a popular
American soprano who went on to become general manager of
the New York City Opera.

Once they cheer the deaths you've amassed
above the orchestra
you've got to choose:

earn adulation

ev'ry

time

you open

your

mouth

or make do
with an ordinary love

Bing cut Callas but left her
a career

To say publicly
the time for being polite was over

To have risen to your position
from a carpenter's apprentice

who witnessed for decades
what we were called how

we were treated
from the bottom up

This had to be an inside-
out job

after Metropolitan Opera General Manager Joseph Volpe's
firing of soprano Kathleen Battle, February 1994

Zeffirelli was blamed
for weighing her down

Bodice: Elizabethan
Neck: Oriental
Headdress: Egyptian

But a queen isn't easily moved

Her subjects must animate
the black-gold motion
of her kingdom

The lighting cue got fucked
so she entered unseen
but her *immortal longings*—

Darling!—in darkness a flare
and I wanted to see my dancers
I did

The happening of her however
black mantis in full glide

Goddamn

Alvin Ailey (January 5, 1931–December 1, 1989) was a noted
dancer, choreographer, activist and founder of Alvin Ailey
American Dance Theater.

I own a flat in Rome with seven nuns as neighbors
I nicknamed my two favorites

Sister Temperance always said *I really shouldn't*
as I filled her third glass

Sister Prudence said cloistering my voice
didn't mean closing my legs

Roma spelled backwards is amor, my dear!
That quote attributed to me

A healthy sex life. Best thing in the world
for a woman's voice

That was Sister Prudence

Without the devils in me
I'd never have arrived here
a trail of carcasses of the many-eyed *been*

My contraband sound
not just for a time

⧼ Self-Portrait as LP

Pressed
labeled and spun
A needle rides
the pitch-dark
of passage
the immortal black
of memory

UNITED STATES GOVERNMENT

TO: DIRECTOR, FBI   DATE: JANUARY 14, 1964
FROM: FIELD AGENT
RE: LEONTYNE PRICE

Confidential Informant T-3, in a report dated
January 12, 1964, advised that popular Negro
singer LEONTYNE PRICE attended a production
of "The Dutchman" by Negro agitator LEROI
JONES, who is married to agitator HETTIE
JONES, a jew. It was staged at PLAYWRIGHTS
UNIT, a theater known for promoting
incendiary work. The play is insolent filth
and undisciplined rage toward the white race.
PRICE endorsed the performance from her seat
in the audience by shouting, "Right on!" and
"Say it!" several times. There was a frenzy
of these outbursts from the Negros in the
audience. PRICE'S involvement with influential
Negros like MARTIN LUTHER KING, JR., ADAM
CLAYTON POWELL, JR., who officiated at her
wedding, and PAUL ROBESON is widely known.
PRICE has also refused to sing to segregated
audiences. It is unknown how far she will go
to support the so-called Negro cause.

Have I talked too much? . . . I've got to watch myself. You know, talking a lot isn't good for a singer.

Leontyne Price

Five encores are not enough
We stomp & beat against our seats

You appear fox-furred
over purple gown

(the politest good-bye
& thank-you)

but the beads can't catch
the light

We cheer until
there's no voice left

after a recital with James Levine,
Metropolitan Opera, March 24, 1985

POSTLUDE

Price retired from the opera stage when she was 57 years old, with no concerning decline in the voice, and continued performing to acclaim in sold-out recitals throughout the 1990s.

I attended one of those recitals my freshman year in college, six years after her first apparition on our kitchen TV. The years that spanned middle and high school, when the floating pavilion of her high C carried me across.

I remember few details of the performance, only that she regaled us inside that modest auditorium as if it were a world-class hall. Her dignity ennobled the very air. After intermission she returned in a gown identical in every way, except color. I want to say it was red.

It would be the first and last time I heard her live.

In the receiving line, I told her I was studying and that she'd been my inspiration. Smiling, she shook my hand and asked, "Are you a Verdian or Mozartean baritone?" I didn't know the difference but said Mozartean (which turned out to be true).

I still count the losses from my time at Vanderbilt, where I was first called "nigger," where the steady, anesthetizing racism of the campus police, professors and classmates poisoned and debilitated me, where I thought I'd *lost* my voice.

Beneath Momma's pained smile when I told her I'd been accepted there, the smile she forced as we unpacked freshman year and when she returned for my recital and graduation: fear.

When do you stop blaming yourself for that feeling of unbelonging? When do you realize that you weren't maladjusted? When do you finally apprehend that the divergence from the lives of your classmates was predetermined by the color line?

Ever the supplicant, the apprentice, I disavowed myself, my sound.

Four years of disinterested teachers treating me as the affirmative action quota whose inelegant and big-boned sound needed to *heel*. Four years of flight, withdrawal, uncountable small and large destructions.

But what of the indestructible?

Despite the public degradation of my Black voice, it was and remains *unconfiscable*.

Early psychiatry pathologized homosexuality as evidence of an arrested adolescence. Although I haven't made a serious study of this long-discredited claim, I marvel at how my own stunted development, emotionally, sexually and socially, mirrors my musical development.

Music remains pseudosexual for me, and I, long practiced in failure, am a defective instrument.

After graduation, with a technique that left a voice nearly drained of confidence, I moved to Washington, DC. I'd been working at the front desk of the Sheraton Washington Hotel for a few months when an older Black bellman, who knew I was a musician, told me that nearby Prince George's County was recruiting teachers.

While I taught General Music and conducted the choir at Stephen Decatur Middle School, Price's example began to dim. It came on slow, not as the calamity it was.

For two long years, my primary exposure to classical music was playing CDs of her and Kathleen Battle, alongside "Rapper's Delight" and Des'ree's "You Gotta Be," for impatient 7th and 8th graders.

Only when she appeared periodically in the news would I perceive my depletion, awaiting a description of my life without her in it. Her arrivals were transfusions.

A gift from my partner Albert, her 1996 box collection spanned her entire career. He knew what she'd meant to me. He saw me flailing and thought it could help revive me. We'd met during my doomed relationship with Joe, a lover I'd driven cross-country to live with in San Francisco.

A famed composer, arranger and conductor nearly 20 years my senior, he was a stand-in for Price. His outsize influence ushered in more than a decade of composing, arranging and conducting—all distracting surrogates for singing.

I listened to the box set, not for joy, but as flagellation. I played and replayed "I Wish I Knew How It Would Feel to Be Free," languishing in the ordinariness I'd been trying to outrun since childhood. This jazz ballad—a neo-spiritual with the work-song pulse of an a cappella choir beneath, soundtrack of my fateful inheritance.

> *I wish I knew how*
> *It would feel to be free*
> *I wish I could break*
> *All the chains holding me*
> *I wish I could say*
> *All the things that I should say*
> *Say 'em loud, say 'em clear*
> *For the whole round world to hear*

Nearly 7,000 miles away from the fallout on September 11, 2001, I was lying on my sofa, reading. It was around 10 p.m. A year earlier, not knowing what to do after studying for a generic master's degree in musical arts, I moved to Tono, a remote town in northeastern Japan surrounded by mountains, rivers and rice fields, the place urbanites go for "traditional" Japan, what they call Japan's "hometown."

There I felt safe, unthreatened, calm. I could meander and ponder without the daily fear that a white person would draw me into their own terror. I thought of James Baldwin, who left New York for Paris and, like me, experienced what neither of us could in the country of our birth: repose.

Arriving in Japan in my late twenties to teach English and music, I began performing more than ever before and, discovering the aesthetic restraint I'd longed for, wrote to distill and clarify my new life.

GEOGRAPHY

I'm at a bar slash Middle Eastern novelty store slash coffee house in northern Japan. Tsuyoshi, the bartender, is quiet. Together, we fit no stereotype. We're alone. An African statue leans against the wall (a woman with breasts like bananas, a small drum in her belly). Ice melts as Lady Day simmers overhead.

Tsuyoshi's drying glasses and wondering about me, why I would bring my body all this way and sit across from him and the glasses he's setting down like chess pieces. He's wondering why I'd come to live in a small town only to be misunderstood: the language gathering in my throat like the sound of dead beetles crunching underfoot.

Less than a month after 9/11, Price emerged from retirement to open the Richard Tucker Foundation's annual gala. With the orchestra standing behind her, clad in black as she was, Price sang "God Bless America" to commemorate the victims.

Her a cappella reading evoked the bugled melancholy of "Taps" but with a matriarchal consolation overwhelming in its stately resolve. When she made the octave leap on "sweet home," it seemed that the audience erupted not only to rally themselves but to cheer the monument before them. She was 74 years old.

During the 2007 Opera News Award tribute, where she was being honored, she absolutely wrecked the unsuspecting crowd with an excerpt of the song "Homing," soaring to the high A of the original key. She was 80 years old.

When I saw the clip, I was in San Francisco, working part-time at an independent bookstore. I'd recently completed a PhD in music education at the University of South Carolina, only to realize that a terminal degree would be, for me, exactly that. I sought out life as a poet.

Mad for Meat, my first collection, came three years later and, amid poems about castrati, a sex club in Thailand, and Aunt Jemima, was one addressed to La Divina Pri-ce.

UPON HEARING LEONTYNE PRICE ON THE UNITED NEGRO COLLEGE FUND COMMERCIAL

I ignored the boys who called me sissy
sang loudly in an operatic voice all the commercials
the theme from *Good Times*
Donna Summer too
But my spine lengthened the night I heard you open
the black fan of your voice
on prime time
Turbaned goddess of my Zenith
the way God struck your soprano
how you rang
We're not asking for a handout, just a hand!

(No matter I misremembered her hot-combed bouffant.)

A monstre sacré formed and deformed by a monstrous business, what did it cost her, a Black woman who traveled uncountable distances—from a southern family without much education or financial resources to the world's most coveted stages? On the wing of a European form never before so closely associated with a Black singer?

Can you talk about the difficulties you faced in your life?

Achievement has nothing except what it's supposed to be. It has no color, it has no religion, it has you and your God-given talent . . . Never let anything negative be in the way of your focus to achieve . . . It is so boring to hear people whine about "everything is so hard." No, thank you. I'm not the person to do that because difficulties are rather private, I think.

She won't answer. Her unflappable bearing remains impenetrable, off limits.

To recount slights, big or small, would sully her story, diminish her *Americanness* that she's declaimed repeatedly. How could she respond to something as terrible as this:

> *A great diva, basking in the twilight of a long career, was singing Tosca one night at the Met in 1961. Before the performance, her dresser asked if she had yet heard Leontyne Price, who had just made a sensational debut as Leonora in "Il Trovatore."*
>
> *The great diva, herself a celebrated if fading exponent of the same role, quivered a few chins in lofty disapproval. "Ah, yes," she purred. "Price. A lovely voice. But the poor thing is singing the wrong repertory!"*
>
> *The dresser registered surprise. "What repertory should Price be singing?" he asked.*
>
> *The great diva smiled a knowing smile. "Bess," she purred. "Just Bess."*

She makes pronouncements: "The color of my skin or the kink of my hair or the spread of my mouth has nothing to do with what you are listening to." Why does she vanquish Blackness from her sound?

I refused to believe she'd said this until I confirmed the source, *Time* magazine (1985). Yet I only had to go back 24 years earlier in the same publication to read the other line she'd drawn:

> *I am not a crusader in anything except my career.*

I thought this settled it but what of the 1976 interview in *Opera News*:

> *But the thing I'm really proudest of is that during all my years of experience, I have not in the process lost any of the original timbre of my voice, which is very dark, very dunkel, in the tender sense. And when I say dark, I mean a black sound. In other words—to be perfectly frank, and this can be taken several ways, and I don't really care—I don't sound white. I guess that's what I'm trying to say, and to me that's worth the whole trip.*

Leontyne Price, acclaimed opera singer, in response to criticism that she has not been active enough in the Black struggle:

> *How can anyone say I could have taken a more active role? What right do I have as a famous singer to speak out politically? I have had to seek the advice of Whitney Young and Roy Wilkins to find my own truths. How could I have been politically involved when my own knowledge was fragmentary? I don't have to prove anything to anyone. I have my own way of expressing my involvement . . .*

Price's artistry is her only absolute. Watch her interviews to witness a remarkable singer—thoroughly guarded and self-conscious—twist into cliché, incoherence and aloofness.

The rolled *r*'s, the European words and phrases dropped whole into a homespun molasses sound accented as if she'd never left Laurel, as if impersonating a diva. It's full-on drag.

Her voice—alive in memory, on vinyl, plastic or digital file—had long ago sealed our devotion. We come for the voice but also for the fevered delirium of her own mythology. She knows this.

For us, she plays the wooden, turban-helmeted and ceremoniously repellent diva who's also disarmingly warm, self-deprecating, bracing.

As soprano Grace Bumbry put it to me about how she and others regarded Price's carrying-on decades ago: "That voice excused everything."

Opera has a particular density—every syllable of every word sung, assigned rhythm, pitch, duration and volume. Perhaps the most fastidious melodrama, it's essentially sport—bloodless, but sport, nonetheless. Outlandishly overdressed singers (who rarely, if ever, resemble their characters) crank out impossibly extreme voices in competition with upwards of 100 instrumentalists.

Opera performances are athletic matches where half the fun is keeping score, being awed by how expertly the outnumbered player-singer overcomes the odds.

Mastering the technique is one thing. Capturing and retaining the attention of conductors, opera houses, impresarios and, most importantly, the public, is another. Sustaining a career over decades—in such a rarefied and taxing art form—is achieved by very few.

We're taught that the correct past tense of sing isn't *singed*, that it's another word altogether. But to sing is to *singe*, to scorch. What must that mean for a singer pushed to the extremes of opera?

Mr. Baptiste straddled me on his living room sofa, pushed his hands into my stomach, said something about connecting me to my breath, that my pants had to be unbuttoned. He did this during a few lessons—I knew it was a compulsion.

Years later, Ms. Ruby, a college friend of Momma's who'd had a distinguished opera career in Germany and had also been his student, said, "Honey, he did it to all the boys. I wondered if he'd done it to you."

This teacher, this husband and father, initiated me into a shadow life. It'd been done to him, I'm sure. Back then, wasn't it usually a teacher, the man across the street? Inside a bathroom stall, under the porch? A rite of passage for a queer boy?

That one time he worried he'd gone too far—when he'd told me to drop my pants so he could see if I "correctly" tightened and loosened my anus to "support the breath," when he called Momma to explain that maybe I'd "misunderstood," when she and Aunt Trina asked if he'd done "anything," when I said no.

Kevin, Kevin, Kevin.

I saw in Price how to abdicate the burden of my own life, to correct my misalignment, to evacuate my child self, my teen self, my young adult self to safety.

My adoration for her exceeded its cause, became afterimage, distortion. Not because of the circumstances of *her* sound, but because of what I thought it could mean for *my* sound.

Later I examined her as an artist, a designation she affixed to herself in interview after interview. She was no performer. She didn't *entertain*, unless it was at her delphinium-blue and avocado accented Greenwich Village home that once belonged to the third vice president, slaveholder Aaron Burr.

Artists must be in conflict with something. Black people are in conflict with the white world. And Black Americans *war* against the mythic deceptions of "unalienable Rights . . . Life, Liberty, the pursuit of Happiness."

Bruises surface where these stingers sting.

I seldom practice yet do occasionally sing in public—my vibrato unwieldy, a wobble. But the color remains.

"Why didn't you sing more?" They always ask.

I didn't sacrifice myself to the discipline because I believed I'd already been born into great deficit, far behind the starting line—where the privileged fallen seemed to begin their normal, heterosexual lives. Surely if there were any truth to the Sermon on the Mount, any recompense for the years of beseeching God to deliver me from my "struggle," I was owed a voice to inhabit without shame.

I'd sought shelter, and when I couldn't find any, sought visibility over acceptance, incoherence over openness, to show everyone that my ways were not theirs. Grandiosity lit by votives of poise and taste, staged as if they'd *produced* me. I was the production.

Vanderbilt seemed cosmopolitan, correct. If anyone could prepare me for the world of opera—that whitest of white worlds—it'd be my white professors who moved with such detached certainty and cool nonchalance. The more they discouraged my Black sound, the more I doubted what my first teachers had instilled in me. I never discerned that attempting to retain my Black sound put me in an adversarial relationship with my professors.

Without Ms. Seals and Mr. Baptiste, I had no one pushing and supporting me to become an opera singer, or *operatic*.

Regret became my most reflexive and muscular emotion, the focusing instrument to know what someone or something means in relation to me, and me to the world.

Whenever I hear or think of her, I regret I'll never make sound others can hardly bear, which is an agony and a consolation.

Price once said that *Prima Donna, Volume 5: Great Soprano Arias from Handel to Britten* is her favorite recording. It features "Casta Diva," an aria famously associated with Maria Callas, one of her inspirations.

"Callas expresses the torture of her life through her voice. Leontyne expresses her joy," said a colleague who'd worked with both.

Price's sound is Black sound—tortured *and* joyous.

That's how I hear: Her.

NOTES

3 Anthony Tommasini, "Aida Takes Her Story to Harlem: Leontyne Price Reads Her Book and Sings for Schoolchildren," *New York Times*, May 30, 2000, E1.

4 Quoted in William Warfield, *William Warfield: My Music and My Life*, with Alton Miller (Champaign, IL: Sagamore Publishing, 1991), 151.

5 Mary Campbell, "Leontyne Price Leaves Opera on a High Note," Associated Press, January 4, 1985, https://www.youtube .com/watch?v=ckrQy6IaEjI.

28 Francesco Lamperti (born March 11, 1811 or 1813–May 1, 1892) attributed this quote to the famous castrato Gaspare Pacchierotti (May 21, 1740–October 28, 1821).

44 James Baldwin, *The Fire Next Time* (New York: Vintage, 1993), 42.

49   Mendi Obadike created the term *acousmatic blackness*. Found in "Low Fidelity: Stereotyped Blackness in the Field of Sound" (PhD diss., Duke University, 2005).

50   Richard Miller, *Solutions for Singers: Tools for Performers and Teachers* (New York: Oxford University Press, 2004), 105.

50   Nina Sun Eidsheim, "Voice as a Technology of Selfhood: Towards an Analysis of Racialized Timbre and Vocal Performance" (PhD diss., University of California San Diego, 2008), 33.

54   Arthur Jafa in discussion with Stephen Best, December 12, 2018, Berkeley Art Museum and Pacific Film Archive, https://www.youtube.com/watch?v=FcIBS015EIQ.

65   Antonin Scalia, "The Disease as Cure: 'In Order to Get Beyond Racism, We Must First Take Account of Race,'" *Washington University Law Review* 1 (1979): 67.

67   This is not an official FBI file. The content, however, is fact.

69 Samuel Chotzinoff, *A Little Night Music: Intimate Conversations with Jascha Heifitz, Vladimir Horowitz, Gian-Carlo Menotti, Leontyne Price, Richard Rodgers, Artur Rubinstein, Andrés Segovia* (New York: Harper & Row, 1964), 94–95.

74 "Saints in Cellophane," *Time*, February 19, 1934, Music, 35, http://content.time.com/time/subscriber/article/0,33009,746990,00.html.

74 W. J. Henderson, "American Opera Keeps Struggling," *American Mercury*, May 1934, 104–5, https://www.unz.com/print/AmMercury-1934may-00104/.

75 Bernard H. Haggin, *Music and Ballet, 1973–1983* (New York: Horizon Press, 1984), 105–6.

76 Photograph by Alfred Eisenstaedt, The LIFE Picture Collection, January 27, 1961 (misdated January 26). Getty Images. Editorial #50530412, Object Name: 759669.

78 Dianne Brooks, "'They Dig Her Message': Opera, Television, and the Black Diva" in *Hop on Pop: The Politics and Pleasures of Popular Culture*, ed. Henry Jenkins, Tara McPherson, and Jane Shattuc (Durham, NC: Duke University Press, 2002), 308. Cited in article notes: Letter from Mrs. William Jordan Rapp to Sylvester Weaver, Wisconsin Historical Society—NBC Papers, box 169, folder 1.

88 James Sandifer, *Porgy and Bess: An American Voice* (University of Michigan, 1998), DVD.

91 Bruce Burroughs, "Indian Summer: Marian Anderson Profile," *Opera News* 69, no. 3 (2004): 62.

93 This is not an official FBI file. The content, however, is fact.

94 Leontyne Price, interview with John Callaway, *Callaway Interviews*, episode 406, May 13, 1981, https://mediaburn.org/video/callaway-interviews-leontyne-price-episode-no-406/.

97 Chotzinoff, *A Little Night Music*, 93–94.

103 Leontyne Price, interview with John Callaway, May 13, 1981.

108 White House memorandum, October 4, 1979, Office of Staff Secretary, Presidential Files, Jimmy Carter Presidential Library and Museum, Atlanta, folder 10/6/79 [1], container 134.

110 James Baldwin and R. H. Darden in conversation, April 1, 1968, KPFK, Los Angeles, BB4514 Pacifica Radio Archives, 60 min., https://archive.org/details/BaldwinAndDarden1968.

116 Illinois Commission on the Status of Women, "Report and Recommendations to the Governor and the General Assembly," 1985, 95.

126 Quote widely attributed to Price.

129 This is not an official FBI file. The content, however, is fact.

130 Chotzinoff, *A Little Night Music*, 95.

140 Billy Taylor and Dick Dallas, "I Wish I Knew," recorded Nov. 12, 1963 on *Right Here, Right Now!* Capitol ST-2039, album issued 1964.

147 "National Endowment for the Arts Opera Honors: Interview with Leontyne Price," June 4, 2010, https://www.arts.gov/stories/video/nea-opera-honors-interview-leontyne-price.

148 Martin Bernheimer, "Yes, but Are We Really Color Deaf?" *Los Angeles Times*, February 17, 1985, L50.

149 Michael Walsh and Nancy Newman, "What Price Glory, Leontyne! The Prima Donna Assoluta Sings Her Last Operatic Role," *Time*, January 14, 1985, 67.

149 "A Voice Like a Banner Flying," *Time*, March 10, 1961, 63.

149 Stephen E. Rubin, "Price on Price," *Opera News*, March 6, 1976, 17.

150 "Words of the Week," *Jet*, February 13, 1975, 30.

151 Grace Bumbry in an interview with Kevin Simmonds, July 11, 2018.

161 "A Voice Like a Banner Flying," *Time*, March 10, 1961, 59.